THE
PROCRASTINATOR'S

guide to

TIME
MANAGEMENT

STEPHEN BROWN

INTRODUCTION

What is time management?

Before we dive into the nitty gritty of techniques to manage time, let's first understand what exactly is time management. Once we have a good understanding of what time management is we can then move on to how to become better at it. So let's go!

Time management is nothing but the process of planning, organizing, and controlling how you spend your time in order to achieve specific goals and objectives. It involves setting priorities, creating a schedule, and managing tasks and activities in an efficient and effective manner.

Good time management can help you use your time more effectively, increase your productivity, and reduce stress and anxiety. Now, who doesn't want that?! It can also help you achieve a better work-life balance, allowing you to make time for both your professional and personal commitments. Time management involves making conscious decisions about how you spend your time, rather than simply reacting to the demands of the moment. It requires self-discipline and the ability to prioritize tasks and responsibilities in order to make the most of your time.

Effective time management involves setting specific goals and objectives, and then organizing and prioritizing your tasks and activities in a way that helps you achieve those goals. This may involve creating a schedule or calendar to plan out your time, breaking larger tasks into smaller, more manageable chunks, and delegating tasks to others when appropriate. Time management also involves being mindful of the way you spend your time and identifying and eliminating activities that are not productive or necessary. This may include setting boundaries to minimize distractions and interruptions and learning to say "no" to unreasonable or unnecessary requests for your time.

Effective time management also requires being aware of your own personal productivity patterns and finding strategies that work best for you. For example, some people may be more productive in the morning, while others may work better at night. It's important to find a schedule and routine that works best for you and your personal needs and goals.

In addition to helping you achieve your goals and be more productive, good time management can also help reduce stress and improve your overall sense of well-being. By taking control of your time and avoiding feeling overwhelmed or overburdened, you can create more balance and harmony in your life.

Why is effective time management important?

Effective time management is essential for both personal and professional success. I am sure you understand this deeply, otherwise, why would you be reading this book :)
By organizing and prioritizing your tasks and activities, you can use your time more efficiently and effectively and achieve your goals more quickly and with less stress.

Professional Life

Effective time management is crucial to achieving success in one's professional life. Good time management allows individuals to prioritize tasks, increase productivity, and improve overall job performance. In this context, effective time management involves planning, prioritizing, and organizing work activities in a way that maximizes productivity and minimizes wasted time.

One key benefit of effective time management is increased productivity. With proper planning and organization, individuals can better focus on important tasks, rather than getting bogged down by less important ones. This helps to increase efficiency and productivity, which can lead to a more successful career.

Effective time management also helps individuals to meet deadlines and achieve goals. By setting clear goals and deadlines, individuals can work towards achieving them systematically, without feeling overwhelmed or stressed. This also helps to prevent last-minute rushes, which can lead to errors and missed deadlines.

Another important aspect of effective time management is prioritization. In a professional context, individuals are often faced with numerous tasks, each with different levels of importance and urgency. Effective time management involves identifying the most important tasks and prioritizing them accordingly. This helps individuals to focus on tasks that are critical to their success, and ensure that they are completed in a timely manner.

Effective time management also promotes better work-life balance. By managing their time effectively, individuals can avoid spending excessive hours at work and instead make time for personal activities and responsibilities. This can help to reduce stress, improve mental health, and create a more balanced and fulfilling life outside of work.

In addition, effective time management can lead to increased job satisfaction. When individuals are able to complete their work efficiently and effectively, they feel a sense of accomplishment and fulfillment. This can lead to increased job satisfaction and motivation, as well as a better overall work experience.

Lastly, effective time management can improve career prospects. Individuals who are able to manage their time effectively are often viewed as reliable, productive, and competent. This can lead to opportunities for career advancement, increased responsibility, and higher salaries.

Personal Life

One of the primary benefits of effective time management in our personal lives is that it allows us to prioritize and accomplish the things that matter most to us. By setting clear goals and priorities, we can focus our time and energy on the activities that are most important, whether it is spending time with loved ones, pursuing hobbies and interests, or working on personal development. This, in turn, helps us to feel more fulfilled and satisfied in our personal lives.

Effective time management also allows us to better manage our personal responsibilities and obligations, such as household chores, errands, and appointments. By planning and organizing our time effectively, we can ensure that we have enough time to complete these tasks without feeling overwhelmed or stressed. This can help to reduce our overall stress levels and improve our overall well-being.

Another important benefit of effective time management in our personal lives is that it allows us to take care of ourselves. By scheduling time for self-care activities such as exercise, meditation, or relaxation, we can improve our physical and mental health and increase our overall well-being. Additionally, by making time for self-care, we can also reduce the risk of burnout and improve our ability to handle stress and difficult situations.

Effective time management also allows us to make time for important relationships in our lives, such as spending quality time with family and friends. By prioritizing these relationships and setting aside time for them, we can strengthen our bonds with others and improve our overall happiness and well-being.

In our personal lives, effective time management also helps us to avoid wasting time on unproductive or unnecessary activities. By setting clear goals and priorities, we can identify the activities that are not contributing to our overall happiness or well-being and eliminate them from our schedules. This can help us to feel more focused and productive in our personal lives.

Finally, effective time management in our personal lives can help us to achieve a better work-life balance. By making time for the things that matter most to us, we can reduce the risk of burnout and improve our ability to manage our work responsibilities. This can lead to a more fulfilling and satisfying life overall.

Effective time management is a crucial skill that can help you achieve your goals, both personally and professionally. It requires self-discipline and the ability to set priorities and manage your tasks and activities in an organized and efficient manner. By developing good time management habits, you can make the most of your time and achieve greater success in all areas of your life.

Benefits of good time management

Good time management can provide a wide range of benefits, both personally and professionally. I'm sure some of these are not new to you. We've seen the impact even a small amount of structure and discipline with managing time has on our life. So why not learn about what other impacts good time management can have.

Increased productivity: By organizing and prioritizing your tasks and activities, you can use your time more efficiently and get more done in less time. This is exactly where we get stuck. We have so much to do and don't know where to start so we just procrastinate and the problem just becomes bigger. Instead of getting scared of climbing the entire mountain we need to focus on just taking one step at a time.

Reduced stress: Good time management can help you avoid feeling overwhelmed or overburdened, which can reduce stress and improve your overall sense of well-being. By setting clear priorities and managing your time effectively, you can take control of your workload and avoid feeling rushed or pressured. This tags along with the first point. Once we start getting work done and figure out a way in which we can get it done we just feel more in control. This automatically reduces your stress which further allows you to work much better.

Better work-life balance: Effective time management can help you balance your various commitments and responsibilities, and make time for the things that are most important to you. Have you missed your kid's dance or dinner with college friends only because you had a lot of work to finish? The biggest goal of good time management is to allow you to do much more with your life. To give you the freedom to explore more parts of your life without the guilt that you are neglecting another part of your life.

Improved goal achievement: By setting clear and specific goals and organizing your time and tasks in a way that helps you achieve those goals, you can make steady progress toward your objectives.

Better reputation: In the professional world, good time management can help you build a good reputation and advance in your career. By consistently meeting deadlines and completing projects on time, you can demonstrate your reliability and dependability to your colleagues and superiors.

Increased creativity and problem-solving skills: Good time management can help free up mental energy and space, allowing you to think more creatively and effectively solve problems. By avoiding feeling overwhelmed or rushed, you can more easily access your creative problem-solving abilities.

ASSESSING YOUR CURRENT TIME MANAGEMENT SKILLS

The first step to improving is to clearly identify the problem. The greater the clarity you age with what exactly is causing your time management problems, the easier it is for you to solve. Assessing your current time management skills involves evaluating how you currently spend your time and identifying any areas that may be hindering your productivity and effectiveness. This may involve tracking your time and measuring how you spend it, identifying common time-wasters, and setting goals for improving your time management.

To assess your current time management skills, you may want to consider questions such as: Do you have clear goals and priorities? Do you use a schedule or calendar to plan out your time? Do you regularly complete tasks on time, or do you tend to procrastinate? Do you have difficulty managing distractions and interruptions? By answering these and other questions, you can get a better understanding of your current time management skills and identify areas for improvement.

Identifying common time wasters

Identifying common time wasters can be an important step in improving your time management skills. Time wasters are activities or habits that consume your time without providing any real value or benefit. They can be a major drain on your productivity and effectiveness and can make it difficult to achieve your goals and objectives. Some common time wasters include:

Checking email and social media: Constantly checking email and social media can be a major distraction and can consume a large amount of your time. Time-wasting by email may seem counter-intuitive. Your work needs you to check your email. How can that be considered time-wasting?! We end up wasting time by not working on our work emails but by getting distracted by all the offers that our inbox is bombarded by. It's not always easy to not make full use of that 15% discount coupon waiting in our inbox. Social Media is a totally different beast. Instagram, YouTube, TikTok, Snapchat, Facebook, etc are made to distract you and keep you distracted Just learning how much time we spend on each of these platforms goes a long way in working towards reducing our usage.

Multitasking: While it may seem like multitasking can help you get more done in less time, it can actually be a major time waster. Switching between tasks can be time-consuming and can decrease your overall productivity. It prevents you from focusing on one job and actually finishing the job. Instead, you are always doing multiple jobs at the same time and none of the jobs on your to-do list are being ticked off. Finishing a job and removing it from your to-do list is incredibly satisfying and pushes you to get more done.

Meetings: "Well this could have just been an email" Unfortunately we have felt this innumerable times while sitting in yet another long and pointless meeting. Meetings can be an important part of work, but they can also be a major time waster if they are not well-organized and productive. Just like any other task if a meeting does not have a pre-defined goal and time deadline it will just drag on and will mostly not be effective. Consider limiting the number of meetings you attend, and be sure to prepare for and follow up on meetings to make the most of your time.

Perfectionism: Perfectionism is one of the core reasons for procrastination. It can be incredibly difficult to just get done with a task because you don't feel it's good enough. This just leads to more and more tasks piling up leading to so much more stress. Striving for perfection can be a time waster if it leads to constantly revisiting and revising tasks. It's important to find a balance between high-quality work and being efficient with your time.

Disorganization: Disorganization can be a major time waster, as it can make it difficult to find things and can lead to wasted time searching for items or trying to remember what you need to do. By staying organized, you can use your time more efficiently.

By identifying and addressing common time wasters, you can improve your time management skills and be more productive.

Measuring how you currently spend your time

A very big eye-opener for me was when I found out how much time I actually spend on my social media apps on my phone. I was pretty much in denial that I did not use social media a lot. I was not addicted. I could stop whenever I want. The classic addiction mentality. Modern devices have tools that allow you to see how many hours of the day you spend on different apps. You will definitely be surprised by the results. Measuring how you currently spend your time can be a helpful step in improving your time management skills. By tracking your time and understanding where it goes, you can identify areas where you may be wasting time and make changes to be more productive and efficient. There are several different methods you can use to measure how you currently spend your time, including:

Time logs: A time log is a record of how you spend your time throughout the day. To create a time log, you can use a planner, a spreadsheet, or a simple piece of paper. Start by dividing your day into blocks of time, and then record what you do during each block. Be as specific as possible, and include all activities, including work tasks, personal activities, and leisure time.

Time tracking software: There are many software tools available that can help you track and measure your time. These tools can automatically record how you spend your time on your computer or phone and can provide detailed reports on your activity. Some time tracking tools even allow you to categorize your time and track your progress towards specific goals.

Time diaries: A time diary is a detailed record of your daily activities. To create a time diary, you can use a planner or a spreadsheet, or you can simply write down your activities in a notebook. Be sure to record everything you do, including work tasks, personal activities, and leisure time.

Smartphone apps: There are many smartphone apps available that can help you track and measure your time. These apps can automatically record your activity on your phone and can provide detailed reports on how you spend your time. Some apps even allow you to set goals and track your progress toward achieving them. Some popular time-tracking apps include:

Toggl: Toggl is a simple time-tracking app that allows you to track your time and activities on your phone or computer. It provides detailed reports on your time usage and allows you to set goals and track your progress.

RescueTime: RescueTime is a time-tracking app that monitors your activity on your phone and computer, and provides detailed reports on how you spend your time. It also includes features to help you stay focused and avoid distractions.

Timely: Timely is a time-tracking app that allows you to record your time and activities on your phone or computer. It provides detailed reports on your time usage and includes features to help you set goals and track your progress.

Harvest: Harvest is a time-tracking app that allows you to record your time and activities on your phone or computer. It provides detailed reports on your time usage and includes features to help you manage your projects and invoicing.

Time Doctor: Time Doctor is a time-tracking app that allows you to track your time and activities on your phone or computer. It provides detailed reports on your time usage and includes features to help you stay focused and avoid distractions.

Setting goals for improving your time management

Setting goals for improving your time management can be a helpful step in achieving greater productivity and success. By setting clear and specific goals, you can focus your efforts and make steady progress toward improving your time management skills. Some tips for setting goals for improving your time management include:

Start small: It's important to start with small, achievable goals rather than trying to make too many changes at once. By setting small, attainable goals, you can build momentum and confidence, and make it easier to maintain your progress over time.

Be specific: Rather than setting vague or general goals, try to be as specific as possible. For example, instead of setting a goal to "be more organized," set a goal to "spend 30 minutes each day decluttering my desk." Specific goals are easier to measure and track and can help you make more progress.

Make your goals measurable: It's important to set goals that can be measured so you can track your progress and see how you're doing. For example, rather than setting a goal to "spend less time on social media," set a goal to "spend no more than 30 minutes per day on social media." This will allow you to track your progress and see how you're doing.

Set a deadline: By setting a deadline for your goals, you can create a sense of urgency and motivation to make progress. Make sure to choose a deadline that is realistic and achievable, but that also provides a sense of challenge.

Review your progress: It's important to regularly review your progress to see how you're doing and make any necessary adjustments. This may involve tracking your time, measuring your productivity, and looking for areas where you can improve.

By setting clear and specific goals for improving your time management, you can focus your efforts and make steady progress toward improving your productivity and effectiveness. Remember to start small and be specific, and be sure to review your progress regularly to make any necessary adjustments. With time and practice, you can develop good time management habits that will help you achieve your goals and be more successful in both your personal and professional life.

SETTING PRIORITIES
AND GOALS

Setting priorities and goals is an important aspect of effective time management. By setting clear priorities, you can focus your efforts on the tasks and activities that are most important and will have the greatest impact. This can help you avoid wasting time on unnecessary or low-priority tasks and make steady progress toward your goals. To set priorities and goals effectively, it's important to:

Identify your most important tasks and activities: Take some time to consider what tasks and activities are most important to you and will have the greatest impact. These are your highest-priority tasks and should be given the most attention. Now, this may seem very obvious and we usually do this intuitively. The problem arises when there are too many tasks to do this process intuitively. Everything seems important and everything needs to be done NOW!

Slowing down, thinking about the tasks, and putting the tasks down on paper with importance and deadlines is the first step. Once that has been done we can start with the following:

Set specific and achievable goals: Rather than setting vague or general goals, be specific and choose goals that are achievable. This will make it easier to measure your progress and stay motivated.

Create a plan: Once you have identified your priorities and set your goals, create a plan for how you will achieve them. This may involve creating a schedule or calendar to plan out your time, breaking larger tasks into smaller, more manageable chunks, and delegating tasks to others when appropriate.

Review and adjust your priorities and goals regularly: It's important to regularly review your priorities and goals to make sure they are still relevant and aligned with your overall objectives. This may involve adjusting your goals or making changes to your plan as needed.

By setting priorities and goals, you can focus your efforts on the tasks and activities that are most important, and make steady progress toward achieving your objectives. This can help you be more productive and efficient, and allow you to achieve your goals more quickly and with less stress.

The importance of setting clear and specific goals

Setting clear and specific goals is an important aspect of effective time management and goal achievement. By setting clear and specific goals, you can focus your efforts and make steady progress toward achieving what you want. Some of the key benefits of setting clear and specific goals include:

Greater clarity and focus: Clear and specific goals provide a clear direction and focus, helping you stay motivated and on track. By knowing exactly what you want to achieve, you can avoid wasting time on unnecessary or low-priority tasks and stay focused on the things that matter most. You need to have eyes on the prize to have any chance of winning the prize

Easier measurement and tracking: Specific goals are easier to measure and track, which can help you see your progress and stay motivated. By setting goals that are specific and measurable, you can track your progress and see how you're doing, and make any necessary adjustments to stay on track. The more specific the goals the less time you take on figuring out how to complete a goal and the easier it becomes to finish that goal.

Increased motivation and commitment: Clear and specific goals can provide a sense of purpose and motivation, helping you stay committed and focused on achieving what you want. By setting goals that are meaningful and important to you, you can stay motivated and engaged, even when things get tough.

Greater accountability: Specific goals provide a clear standard for measuring your progress, which can increase your accountability and help you stay on track. By setting clear and specific goals, you can hold yourself accountable for making progress and achieving what you want.

Overall, setting clear and specific goals is an important aspect of effective time management and goal achievement. By setting goals that are clear, specific, and measurable, you can focus your efforts and make steady progress towards achieving what you want, and increase your chances of success.

How to break down larger goals into smaller, more manageable tasks

Breaking down larger goals into smaller, more manageable tasks can be an effective way to make progress and achieve what you want. By dividing your goals into smaller, more manageable tasks, you can focus your efforts and make steady progress toward achieving your objectives. Some tips for breaking down larger goals into smaller tasks include:

Start with the end in mind: Before you start breaking down your goals into smaller tasks, it's important to have a clear idea of what you want to achieve. Take some time to think about your larger goals and what you want to accomplish. This will help you identify the smaller tasks that need to be completed in order to achieve your objectives.

Identify the key steps and milestones: Once you have a clear idea of your larger goals, identify the key steps and milestones that will be required to achieve them. These might include research, planning, implementation, and evaluation.

Break down each step into smaller tasks: Once you have identified the key steps and milestones, break each step down into smaller tasks. These might include specific actions or activities that need to be completed in order to make progress.

Prioritize your tasks: Once you have a list of smaller tasks, prioritize them based on their importance and urgency. This will help you focus on the most important tasks first and make sure you are making progress toward your larger goals.

Set deadlines: To stay motivated and on track, it can be helpful to set deadlines for completing each of your smaller tasks. This will help you create a sense of urgency and ensure that you are making progress toward your goals.

Review and adjust as needed: As you work on your smaller tasks, be sure to regularly review your progress and make any necessary adjustments. This may involve revising your list of tasks, setting new deadlines, or adjusting your priorities as needed.

Overall, breaking down larger goals into smaller, more manageable tasks can be an effective way to make progress and achieve what you want. By dividing your goals into smaller tasks, you can focus your efforts and make steady progress toward achieving your objectives.

Techniques for prioritizing tasks

There are many different techniques for prioritizing tasks, and the best approach will depend on your individual needs and goals. Some common techniques for prioritizing tasks include

The Eisenhower Method: The Eisenhower Method is a productivity and time management system that helps individuals prioritize their tasks and activities. It is named after Dwight D. Eisenhower, the 34th President of the United States, who was known for his exceptional productivity and ability to manage multiple responsibilities. The method involves categorizing tasks into four quadrants based on their level of urgency and importance.

Quadrant 1 includes tasks that are both urgent and important, such as deadlines and emergencies, and should be prioritized first.

Quadrant 2 includes tasks that are important but not urgent, such as long-term planning and personal development, and should be given attention after urgent tasks are completed.

Quadrant 3 includes tasks that are urgent but not important, such as interruptions and unnecessary meetings, and should be delegated or minimized.

Quadrant 4 includes tasks that are neither urgent nor important, such as distractions and time-wasting activities, and should be avoided or minimized as much as possible.

The Eisenhower Method encourages individuals to focus on tasks that are important rather than simply urgent, as this can help prevent burnout and increase overall productivity. By prioritizing tasks based on their level of urgency and importance, individuals can effectively manage their time and achieve their goals more efficiently.

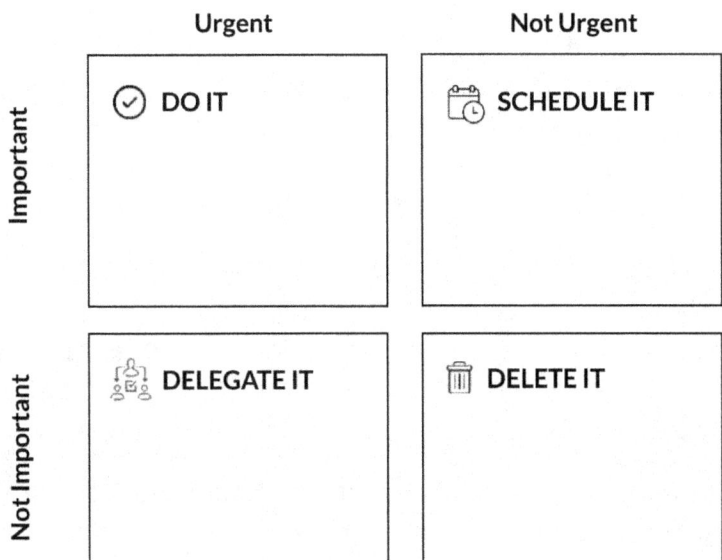

The ABC Method: The ABC method is a technique for prioritizing tasks based on their level of importance and urgency. The method was popularized by Brian Tracy in his book "Eat That Frog!" and is widely used in time management and productivity strategies. The ABC method involves categorizing tasks into three categories: A, B, and C.

Tasks that are categorized as A are those that are the most important and urgent, and must be done immediately. These are tasks that have consequences if they are not completed, and can have a significant impact on one's goals and objectives.

Tasks that are categorized as B are important but not as urgent as A tasks. These tasks should be completed as soon as possible after A tasks have been completed.

Tasks that are categorized as C are tasks that are neither important nor urgent. These tasks should be delegated or eliminated if possible, as they can be distractions from more important tasks.
An important aspect of the ABC method is to further prioritize A tasks by assigning them a numerical value based on their level of importance. For example, an A1 task is more important than an A2 task, which is more important than an A3 task.

The Pareto Principle: The Pareto Principle, also known as the 80/20 rule, is a popular concept in time management and productivity. The principle states that 80% of the effects come from 20% of the causes. Applied to time management, this means that 80% of your results will come from 20% of your activities. In other words, by focusing on the most important 20% of your tasks, you can achieve 80% of your desired results.

To apply the Pareto Principle to time management, it's important to identify the most important tasks that will have the biggest impact on your goals. These are often the tasks that require the most time, effort, or creativity. By prioritizing these tasks and focusing on them first, you can make sure that you are spending your time and energy where it will have the most impact.

Another way to apply the Pareto Principle is to identify the tasks that are consuming the most time without adding significant value. These are often the low-priority tasks that can be delegated, automated, or eliminated altogether. By focusing on the tasks that provide the most value and eliminating the tasks that don't, you can free up more time and energy to focus on the tasks that really matter.

One potential challenge of the Pareto Principle is that it can be difficult to determine which tasks are the most important. It's important to take the time to reflect on your goals and priorities and to seek feedback from others to help you identify the tasks that will have the biggest impact. Additionally, it's important to be flexible and adaptable, as priorities can shift over time and what was once a high-priority task may no longer be as important.

Overall, the Pareto Principle can be a valuable tool for time management and productivity. By focusing on the tasks that provide the most value and eliminating the tasks that don't, you can make the most of your time and achieve your goals more efficiently.

SCHEDULING AND
TIME BLOCKING

Scheduling and time blocking are techniques that involve setting aside dedicated blocks of time for specific tasks and activities. Scheduling involves creating a calendar or schedule that outlines when you will work on different tasks and activities, while time blocking involves setting aside specific blocks of time for specific tasks. By scheduling and time blocking, you can better manage your time and increase your productivity.

Techniques for time blocking

Time blocking is a technique for managing your time by setting aside dedicated blocks of time for specific tasks and activities. It allows you to divide large chunks of work into smaller achievable parts and assign time for each chunk. This allows you to fully focus on the specific Some techniques for time blocking include:

Identify your priorities: Before you start time blocking, it's important to identify your most important tasks and activities. These are the tasks that should be given the highest priority and should be scheduled first. We can use the methods we discussed earlier to set priorities to tasks such as the Eisenhover method, ABC method, etc

Determine the length of your time blocks: Next, determine how long you want your time blocks to be. Some people find it helpful to schedule shorter blocks of time, such as 30-60 minutes, while others prefer longer blocks, such as 90-120 minutes. The key is to find a length that works best for you and allows you to stay focused and productive.

Schedule your time blocks: Once you have identified your priorities and determined the length of your time blocks, start scheduling your time. Be sure to include time for breaks and rest, as well as time for unexpected tasks or interruptions.

Avoid multitasking: During your time blocks, try to focus on one task at a time. Avoid multitasking or switching between tasks, as this can decrease your productivity and make it harder to stay focused.

Adjust as needed: As you start time blocking, you may find that you need to adjust your schedule or time blocks to better meet your needs and goals. Be flexible and willing to make adjustments as needed to find a time-blocking system that works best for you.

Time blocking is a powerful technique for managing your time and increasing your productivity. By setting aside dedicated blocks of time for specific tasks and activities, you can stay focused and on track, and make the most of your day.

The benefits of creating a schedule or calendar

Creating a schedule or calendar can be a powerful tool for managing time and increasing productivity. Some of the benefits of creating a schedule or calendar include

Better organization: A schedule or calendar can help you stay organized by providing a clear overview of your tasks and activities. By keeping track of your schedule and calendar, you can avoid double-booking or forgetting important tasks.

Greater efficiency: By creating a schedule or calendar, you can be more efficient by allocating your time and resources wisely. By planning out your tasks and activities in advance, you can work more efficiently and achieve your goals more quickly.

Enhanced goal achievement: By creating a schedule or calendar, you can make steady progress toward achieving your goals. By setting deadlines and breaking your goals down into smaller tasks, you can focus your efforts and make steady progress toward achieving what you want.

Improved time management: A schedule or calendar can help you better manage your time by outlining when you will work on specific tasks and activities. By having a clear plan for how you will allocate your time, you can avoid wasting time and stay on track.

Increased productivity: By creating a schedule or calendar, you can be more productive by focusing on specific tasks at specific times. This can help you avoid distractions and stay focused on what you're working on, allowing you to get more done in less time.

Creating a schedule or calendar can be a powerful tool for managing your time and increasing your productivity. By outlining your tasks and activities in advance, you can stay organized, focused, and efficient, and make steady progress toward achieving your goals.

How to balance structured and flexible time

Balancing structured and flexible time can be an effective way to manage your time and increase your productivity. Structured time refers to the blocks of time you have scheduled for specific tasks and activities, while flexible time refers to the blocks of time you have available for unexpected tasks or interruptions. Some tips for balancing structured and flexible time include:

Identify your priorities: Before you start balancing your structured and flexible time, it's important to identify your most important tasks and activities. These are the tasks that should be given the highest priority and should be scheduled first.

Schedule your structured time: Once you have identified your priorities, start scheduling your structured time. This might include blocks of time for specific tasks, meetings, and appointments. Be sure to include breaks and rest in your schedule as well.

Leave room for flexibility: While it's important to have a structured schedule, it's also important to leave room for flexibility. This might include blocks of time for unexpected tasks or interruptions, or time for rest and relaxation.

Be willing to adjust your schedule: As you start balancing your structured and flexible time, you may find that you need to adjust your schedule to better meet your needs and goals. Be flexible and willing to make adjustments as needed to find a balance that works best for you.

Set boundaries: To effectively balance your structured and flexible time, it's important to set boundaries and protect your time. This might involve saying no to non-essential tasks or setting limits on how much time you spend on certain activities.

Balancing structured and flexible time can be an effective way to manage your time and increase your productivity. By scheduling blocks of time for specific tasks and activities, and leaving room for flexibility and unexpected tasks, you can find a balance that works best for you and your goals.

OVERCOMING
PROCRASTINATION

If you have reached here I am sure you know what procrastination is. I wanted to write about procrastination earlier but I just put if off

Procrastination can be caused by a variety of factors, such as lack of motivation, difficulty with time management, or fear of failure. It's not the easiest thing to get over and the first step to getting over it is just being kind to yourself. We know that procrastination reduces productivity and increases stress.

We are going to first understand the cause of procrastination and then how we can overcome it.

What causes procrastination?

There are several reasons why we procrastinate though the biggest reason is perfectionism.

Perfectionism

Now that may seem counter intuitive. How can trying to do your job well lead to not being able to complete your job?! This is why it's important to understand perfectionism. Perfectionism is not just the tendency of doing your job well it's a tendency to set high standards for oneself and others, and to strive for flawlessness in one's work. The extremely high standards are almost unachievable pushing you to just give up the task.

One of the ways perfectionism leads to procrastination is through the fear of failure. We set such high standards for ourselves that feel that we cannot begin a task until we are confident we can complete it perfectly. This leads to a reluctance to start the task, as well as to prolonged periods of procrastination. Additionally, we may become so focused on minor details that we lose sight of the bigger picture, which causes us to become stuck or overwhelmed.

Perfectionism can also lead to procrastination through the tendency to overthink or overanalyze. We are often highly self-critical and spend too much time thinking about all the ways we could fail or all the things we need to do to succeed. This can lead to analysis paralysis, or a situation in which we becomes so overwhelmed with options or possibilities that we are unable to take action.

Finally, perfectionism can cause procrastination through the tendency to avoid tasks that are perceived as boring or unimportant. We may prioritize tasks that are more challenging or interesting, even if they are not the most important or time-sensitive tasks. This can lead to procrastination on the less interesting tasks, which may be put off until the last minute or even ignored altogether.

Fear of failure

Fear of failure can be a major cause of procrastination. When we fear that we might not be able to complete a task to the best of our ability or that we might fail in some way, it can be tempting to put off the task altogether. This fear can be especially strong if we attach our self-worth to the outcome of the task or if we believe that others will judge us based on our performance.

The fear of failure can create a vicious cycle of procrastination. As we delay working on the task, the deadline approaches and the pressure to perform increases, which can lead to even more anxiety and fear. This, in turn, can cause us to avoid the task even more, leading to even more stress and anxiety.

Perfectionism and fear of failure often go hand in hand. When we have high standards for ourselves and fear that we won't meet those standards, it can be easy to get stuck in a cycle of procrastination. This is because we may feel that if we can't do something perfectly, it's not worth doing at all. In reality, however, most tasks don't require perfection, and sometimes it's better to complete a task imperfectly than to not complete it at all.

To overcome the fear of failure and avoid procrastination, it can be helpful to reframe our thoughts and focus on progress rather than perfection. Instead of aiming for perfection, we can set more realistic goals and focus on making progress towards those goals. We can also challenge our negative thoughts and remind ourselves that making mistakes and experiencing setbacks is a natural part of the learning process. Additionally, we can try to cultivate a growth mindset, where we see challenges as opportunities for growth and learning rather than as threats to our self-worth. By changing our mindset and focusing on progress rather than perfection, we can overcome the fear of failure and break the cycle of procrastination.

Low self-esteem

Low self-esteem can also be a contributing factor to procrastination. People who struggle with low self-esteem may believe that they are not capable of achieving their goals, and may feel overwhelmed or anxious about taking on new tasks or responsibilities. This can lead to a lack of motivation and a tendency to put things off, as they may feel that there is little point in trying if they believe they will ultimately fail.

Low self-esteem can also make it difficult for people to ask for help or support, which can compound feelings of stress and anxiety, and lead to further procrastination. In some cases, people with low self-esteem may also struggle with perfectionism, as they may feel that they need to complete tasks flawlessly in order to prove their worth or avoid criticism.

To overcome procrastination caused by low self-esteem, it is important to work on building self-confidence and self-efficacy. This can involve setting small, achievable goals, and gradually increasing the difficulty of tasks as you become more comfortable and confident. It may also involve seeking out support and encouragement from others, whether that be through working with a mentor or coach or seeking feedback from colleagues or friends

Strategies for overcoming procrastination

Procrastination can be incredibly difficult to overcome though not impossible. Let's see how we can get over it. Here are some ways we can go about it.

Identify the underlying causes: Understanding the reasons why you procrastinate can be an important first step in overcoming this tendency. It might be helpful to reflect on what triggers your procrastination and what you are trying to avoid or gain by delaying tasks.

Set clear goals and priorities: Having a clear sense of your goals and priorities can help you stay focused and motivated, and reduce the temptation to procrastinate. Break your goals down into smaller, more manageable tasks, and prioritize them based on their importance and urgency.

Break tasks down into smaller steps: Large, complex tasks can be intimidating and can lead to procrastination. To overcome this, try breaking tasks down into smaller, more manageable steps. This can help you feel more in control and make progress more easily.

Use scheduling and time blocking: Scheduling and time blocking can be helpful tools for managing your time and staying on track. Set aside dedicated blocks of time for specific tasks, and try to avoid multitasking or switching between tasks.

Find accountability: Having someone to hold you accountable for your actions can be a powerful motivator. Consider finding a accountability partner, or joining a group or community that can support and encourage you.

Procrastination requires a combination of self-awareness, goal-setting, and time management skills. By identifying the underlying causes of your procrastination, setting clear goals and priorities, breaking tasks down into smaller steps, and using tools such as scheduling and time blocking, you can overcome this tendency and be more productive.

MANAGING DISTRACTIONS AND INCREASING EFFICIENCY

Managing distractions

We all want to reduce distractions and be more productive though sometimes we get distracted and do not even realize we were distracted till much later. We won't get rid of all our distraction sin one day but we can start by identifying them and then work on reducing them gradually.

There are many different sources of distractions and interruptions, and they can vary depending on your environment, work style, and personal preferences. Some common sources of distractions and interruptions include:

Notifications: Notifications from email, social media, or other apps can be major sources of distraction. These notifications can pull your attention away from what you're working on and make it harder to focus.

The problem with notifications is that they are designed to capture our attention and demand an immediate response. Every time we receive a notification, our brains are distracted from the task at hand, and it takes time and mental effort to refocus our attention and resume our work. Even if we choose to ignore the notification, the mere presence of the alert can create a sense of anticipation and anxiety that can further distract us and decrease our productivity.

Moreover, notifications can trigger the dopamine response in our brain, which is the same chemical reaction that is associated with pleasure and reward. This can create a feedback loop that reinforces our desire to check our devices and respond to notifications, even when they are not essential or urgent.

To minimize the impact of notifications on our productivity, it is important to turn off or reduce non-essential notifications on our devices. This can be done by going into the settings of each app and adjusting the notification preferences. It can also be helpful to schedule specific times to check emails, social media, and other notifications, rather than allowing them to interrupt our work throughout the day.

Another option is to use software tools that can help manage notifications and reduce distractions, such as focus or productivity apps. These apps can block certain types of notifications during specific time periods or provide reminders to take breaks and stay focused on the task at hand.

Just by being mindful of our notification settings and developing strategies to manage them, we can reduce distractions and improve our ability to focus on the important tasks in our lives.

Interruptions from others: Interruptions from others can be a significant source of distractions, especially in the workplace. These interruptions can be in the form of a colleague stopping by your desk to chat, a phone call, or an email notification. They can cause you to lose focus and momentum on the task you were working on, which can lead to lower productivity and increased stress.

One of the reasons why interruptions from others can be so distracting is that they require you to shift your attention away from what you were doing and refocus on the interruption. This can take a significant amount of mental effort, especially if the interruption is unexpected or requires you to switch tasks entirely. It can also take time to get back into the flow of what you were working on before the interruption occurred, further reducing your productivity.

In addition, interruptions from others can lead to a sense of being overwhelmed or overloaded with work. If you are constantly being interrupted throughout the day, it can be challenging to make progress on your most important tasks, which can create a feeling of being behind or overwhelmed.

To minimize interruptions from others, it can be helpful to establish clear boundaries and communicate them effectively. For example, you could let your colleagues know that you are working on an important project and would prefer not to be interrupted unless it is urgent. You could also schedule specific times during the day when you are available for meetings or conversations, and encourage your colleagues to respect these times.

Another effective strategy is to make yourself less available for interruptions by closing your office door or putting on noise-canceling headphones. This sends a signal to others that you are focused and should not be interrupted unless it is absolutely necessary.

Finally, it is important to be proactive in managing your workload and setting priorities. By prioritizing your most important tasks and working on them first, you can reduce the likelihood of being interrupted during critical work periods. Additionally, by setting realistic expectations with colleagues and stakeholders, you can reduce the pressure to constantly be available and responsive, which can help to reduce interruptions and distractions.

Noise and distractions in your environment: Noise and other distractions in your environment can be a significant source of distraction that can disrupt your concentration and lower your productivity. External noise such as traffic, construction, or conversations can be particularly disruptive when you're trying to focus on a task. In addition to noise, other visual distractions in your environment can also be problematic, such as cluttered or disorganized workspaces, frequent movement or activity around you, or even notifications from your devices.

These distractions can lead to a phenomenon known as "attention residue," where your mind continues to focus on the previous task even after it has been completed, preventing you from fully engaging in your current task. This can lead to decreased efficiency and increased stress levels.

To minimize the impact of noise and distractions in your environment, you can try a few strategies. One approach is to try to control your environment as much as possible. This might mean finding a quieter space to work, such as a private office or a library. You can also try wearing noise-cancelling headphones or using apps that generate white noise or other calming sounds to help mask external noises.

Another approach is to practice mindfulness and staying present in the moment. This involves acknowledging the presence of external distractions without allowing them to consume your attention or distract you from your current task. Mindfulness exercises such as deep breathing, meditation, or visualization can help you train your mind to focus more effectively and filter out external distractions.

Finally, you can try to create a distraction-free environment by removing potential sources of distraction or interruptions. This might include turning off notifications on your devices, putting your phone on silent or in a separate room, and limiting your access to social media or other distracting websites while you work. By creating a distraction-free environment and practicing mindfulness, you can improve your ability to focus and increase your productivity.

Personal habits and tendencies: Personal habits and tendencies can cause distractions in several ways. For example, some people have a tendency to multitask, which can lead to decreased productivity and attention to detail. While some people believe that multitasking is an effective way to get more done in less time, research has shown that it can actually decrease productivity by up to 40%

Additionally, some people may have a tendency to procrastinate, which can lead to a lack of motivation and focus. Procrastination can also cause stress and anxiety, which can further distract you from the task at hand. Other personal habits that can cause distractions include perfectionism, which can lead to spending too much time on a task, and impulsivity, which can lead to distractions from impulsive behaviors.

Furthermore, personal distractions such as hunger, fatigue, and physical discomfort can also impact your ability to concentrate and stay focused. For instance, if you are hungry or thirsty, you may find it difficult to focus on a task, as your mind may be preoccupied with thoughts of food or drink. Similarly, if you are experiencing physical discomfort or pain, such as a headache or backache, it can be challenging to focus on your work.

It's important to identify your own personal habits and tendencies that may cause distractions so that you can take steps to mitigate them. For example, if you have a tendency to procrastinate, you might try breaking down tasks into smaller, more manageable steps and setting specific deadlines for each step. If you have a tendency to multitask, try focusing on one task at a time and minimizing distractions in your environment. If you are easily distracted by physical discomfort, make sure you are comfortable before starting a task, and take breaks as needed to stretch and move around.

Understanding your personal habits and tendencies that may cause distractions is an important step in improving your ability to focus and be productive. By taking steps to mitigate these distractions, you can improve your work performance and achieve your goals more efficiently.

There are many different sources of distractions and interruptions, and it can be helpful to identify the specific distractions and interruptions that are impacting your productivity. Once you know what is causing your distractions and interruptions, you can take steps to minimize or eliminate them and improve your focus and productivity.

Strategies for minimizing distractions

Now that we have understood the types of distractions we face on a day to day basis, lets figure out ways in which we can reduce these distractions. Here are some strategies for minimizing distractions:

Set boundaries: To minimize distractions, it can be helpful to set boundaries and protect your time. This might involve setting aside specific blocks of time for focused work, or turning off notifications during these times. Setting boundaries can help you to reduce distractions and increase your productivity. Here are some steps you can take to set boundaries:

Identify your priorities and communicate: Knowing what is most important to you will help you to set boundaries that align with your goals and values. Let others know what your boundaries are and why they are important to you. This can be done in a polite and respectful manner.

Be consistent: Once you have set your boundaries, be consistent in enforcing them. This will help others to take them seriously.

Say no: Learn to say no to requests or tasks that do not align with your priorities or that would interfere with your boundaries.

Use technology to your advantage: You can use technology to set boundaries, such as turning off notifications during certain times of the day or using apps that block certain websites or apps during work hours.

Take breaks: Taking regular breaks can help you to recharge and refocus, which can ultimately increase your productivity and help you to avoid distractions.

Remember that setting boundaries is not selfish, but rather a way to protect your time and energy so that you can be more effective in your work and personal life.

Use tools to block distractions: There are a variety of tools and software that can help you block distractions and stay focused. There are several tools and techniques that can be used to minimize distractions and increase focus. Here are some examples:

Noise-cancelling headphones: These headphones use technology to cancel out external noises and create a more peaceful environment. They may seem very expensive at first but the peace and quiet they provide are invaluable.

Productivity apps: There are many productivity apps available that can help you stay on task and minimize distractions. Some popular options include RescueTime, Forest, and Focus@Will.

Browser extensions: There are several browser extensions that can help to block distracting websites and social media platforms. Examples include StayFocusd and Freedom.

Time management software: Time management software can help you track your time and stay focused on your tasks. Examples include Toggl and Harvest.

Task management tools: These tools can help you stay organized and focused by keeping track of your to-do list and priorities. Examples include Todoist and Trello.

Physical barriers: Setting up physical barriers can help to reduce distractions. For example, closing the door to your office or using a room divider to block out noise and visual distractions.

It's important to note that different tools and techniques work for different people, and it's important to experiment to find what works best for you. Additionally, while tools and techniques can help to minimize distractions, it's also important to address the root causes of distraction, such as personal habits and tendencies, to achieve long-term improvements in focus and productivity.

Create a distraction-free environment: Your physical environment can also be a source of distractions. To minimize distractions, try to create a clean, organized, and quiet workspace. This might involve finding a quiet location to work, or using noise-cancelling headphones to block out noise.

Avoid multitasking: Multitasking can be a major source of distractions, as it involves constantly switching between different tasks and contexts. To minimize distractions, try to focus on one task at a time, and avoid switching between tasks unless it is absolutely necessary.

Communicate with others: If interruptions from other people are a major source of distraction, it can be helpful to communicate your needs and boundaries. This might involve letting others know when you are unavailable, or setting up specific times for meetings or conversations.

Minimizing distractions requires a combination of self-awareness, boundary-setting, and time management skills. By identifying your distractions, setting boundaries, using tools to block distractions, creating a distraction-free environment, avoiding multitasking, and communicating with others, you can minimize the impact of distractions and stay focused on what you need to get done.

Increasing efficiency and productivity

Increasing efficiency and productivity is about maximizing your output and getting more done in less time. Here are some strategies for increasing efficiency and productivity:

Identify your goals: To increase your efficiency and productivity, it's important to know what you're working towards. Clearly define your goals and priorities, and use them as a guide for how you allocate your time and resources.

Break tasks down into smaller steps: Large, complex tasks can be overwhelming and can lead to procrastination. To increase your efficiency, try breaking tasks down into smaller, more manageable steps. This can help you feel more in control and make progress more easily.

Use scheduling and time blocking: Scheduling and time blocking can be helpful tools for managing your time and staying on track. Set aside dedicated blocks of time for specific tasks, and try to avoid multitasking or switching between tasks.

Minimize distractions and interruptions: Distractions and interruptions can be major challenges when it comes to increasing your efficiency and productivity. To minimize these distractions, try setting boundaries, using tools to block distractions, creating a distraction-free environment, and avoiding multitasking.

Take breaks and prioritize self-care: It's important to take breaks and prioritize self-care in order to maintain your energy and focus. Regular breaks can help you recharge and refocus, and taking care of your physical and mental health can help you be more productive overall.

Continuously assess and improve: To increase your efficiency and productivity, it's important to continuously assess and improve your work processes. This might involve seeking feedback from others, experimenting with different approaches, or learning new skills and tools.

Streamlining tasks and workflow

Streamlining tasks and workflow is about finding ways to work more efficiently and effectively, and reducing unnecessary steps or bottlenecks in your process. Here are some techniques for streamlining tasks and workflow:

Identify bottlenecks: Identifying bottlenecks in your workflow can be a helpful way to pinpoint areas where you can improve efficiency and productivity. Here are some steps you can take to identify bottlenecks and streamline your tasks:

Identify the processes: Start by mapping out all the processes involved in the task or project. This may involve breaking down the task into smaller steps or sub-tasks. Once you have a clear understanding of the entire process, you can begin to identify where the bottlenecks are.

Analyze each step: Take a closer look at each step in the process and identify any steps that are taking longer than they should. This could be due to various reasons such as lack of resources, poor communication, or a lack of understanding about the process.

Prioritize the bottlenecks: Once you have identified the bottlenecks, prioritize them based on their impact on the overall process. Some bottlenecks may be more critical than others, so it's important to focus on those that will have the greatest impact on the process.

Develop solutions: After prioritizing the bottlenecks, develop potential solutions for each one. This may involve assigning additional resources to certain steps, improving communication, or streamlining certain processes.

Test the solutions: Once you have developed solutions, test them to see if they are effective. This may involve implementing the solutions on a small scale and monitoring their impact before rolling them out on a larger scale.

<u>Continuously monitor and improve:</u> Once you have implemented the solutions, continue to monitor the process to ensure that the bottlenecks have been eliminated or reduced. If necessary, make further improvements to the process to continue to streamline and improve efficiency.

There are also several tools and techniques that can be used to help identify bottlenecks and streamline tasks, including process mapping, flowcharts, and data analysis tools. These tools can provide a visual representation of the process and help identify areas where improvements can be made.

Automate repetitive tasks: Automating repetitive tasks can be a effective way to streamline your workflow. Automating repetitive tasks can save a significant amount of time and streamline your workflow. Here are some steps you can take to automate tasks:

Identify the tasks that are repetitive and time-consuming: Look for tasks that you perform regularly and take up a lot of your time.

Evaluate the tasks to see which ones can be automated: Some tasks may be too complex or require human input, but others can be automated easily.

Choose the right automation tools: There are many automation tools available, such as Zapier, IFTTT, and Microsoft Power Automate, that can help you automate your tasks.

Create a plan for automation: Determine the sequence of steps that need to be automated and the specific tool or program that you will use for each task.

Test and refine the automation: Once you have set up the automation, test it thoroughly to make sure it is working as intended. Refine the process as needed to ensure optimal efficiency.

Monitor the automation: Regularly check to make sure that the automated tasks are being performed correctly and adjust as needed.

By automating repetitive tasks, you can free up time to focus on other important tasks and achieve greater productivity.

Simplify your processes: Streamlining your tasks and workflow can also involve simplifying your processes. This might involve eliminating unnecessary steps, streamlining communication, or consolidating tasks.

Use templates and standardized documents: Using templates and standardized documents can help you save time and reduce errors by providing a consistent structure for your work. This might include templates for reports, presentations, or other types of documents.

Implement a project management system: Implementing a project management system can help you streamline tasks by providing a structured approach to managing projects and tasks. The system can help you prioritize tasks, set deadlines, and assign responsibilities to team members. Here are some steps to implementing a project management system:

Choose a project management tool: There are several project management tools available, both free and paid. Some popular ones include Trello, Asana, and Monday.com. Choose a tool that best fits your needs.

Define the project: Clearly define the project goals, objectives, and deliverables. Break down the project into smaller tasks and subtasks, and set deadlines for each.

Assign tasks and responsibilities: Assign tasks to team members and set deadlines. Ensure that everyone is clear on their responsibilities and what is expected of them.

Monitor progress: Use the project management tool to monitor progress and track the status of each task. Update the tool regularly to ensure that everyone is up to date.

Communicate: Communication is key to successful project management. Use the project management tool to communicate with team members, share files and documents, and provide feedback.

Evaluate and improve: Once the project is complete, evaluate its success and identify areas for improvement. Use this feedback to improve your project management system for future projects.

Implementing a project management system can take some time and effort, but the benefits are well worth it. It can help you streamline tasks, improve productivity, and ensure that projects are completed on time and within budget.

Seek feedback and continuously improve: To continue streamlining your tasks and workflow, it's important to seek feedback from others and continuously assess and improve your processes. This might involve soliciting feedback from team members, experimenting with new approaches, or learning new skills and tools.

Streamlining tasks and workflow requires a combination of automation, simplification, standardization, and continuous improvement. By identifying bottlenecks, automating repetitive tasks, simplifying your processes, using templates and standardized documents, implementing a project management system, and seeking feedback, you can improve your efficiency and effectiveness and streamline your tasks and workflow.

MAINTAINING WORK
LIFE BALANCE

The importance of maintaining balance between work life and personal life

Work-life balance refers to finding an optimal balance between work responsibilities and personal life responsibilities, such as family, friends, hobbies, and leisure activities. It is the ability to successfully manage the demands and priorities of both work and personal life without one interfering with the other.

One of the main reasons of becoming better at time management is to build this balance. The more efficient we are at work the more time we can spend outside work. The better time management reduces our stress levels that allows us to enjoy our time at work and away much better.

Achieving work-life balance is important because it can improve overall well-being, reduce stress and burnout, increase job satisfaction and productivity, and improve relationships with family and friends. Work-life balance can also lead to a more fulfilling life, allowing individuals to pursue personal interests and hobbies, spend quality time with loved ones, and take care of their physical and emotional health.

However, it is important to note that work-life balance does not necessarily mean that one must spend an equal amount of time between work and personal life. Rather, it is about finding a balance that works for each individual's unique circumstances and priorities. Some people may prioritize work more heavily, while others may prioritize personal life more heavily. The key is to find a balance that works for each individual's needs and priorities, while ensuring that neither work nor personal life is neglected.

Strategies for managing work-life balance

Managing work-life balance is about finding a healthy balance between your professional and personal commitments, and making time for the things that are important to you. Here are some strategies for managing work-life balance:

Set clear boundaries: To manage your work-life balance, it's important to set clear boundaries around your work and personal time. This might involve setting specific hours for work, or setting aside dedicated blocks of time for personal pursuits.

Prioritize your commitments: To manage your work-life balance, it's important to prioritize your commitments and focus on what is most important to you. This might involve setting clear goals and priorities, and saying no to commitments that don't align with your values or goals.

Delegate and outsource tasks: To manage your workload and free up time for other commitments, consider delegating tasks or outsourcing tasks to others. This might involve hiring a virtual assistant or using a task management tool to assign tasks to team members.

Make time for self-care: Self-care is an important aspect of work-life balance, and it's important to make time for activities that nourish your body, mind, and spirit. This might include things like exercising, meditating, or taking breaks to recharge.

Communicate with your employer: If you are having trouble balancing your work and personal commitments, it can be helpful to communicate with your employer. This might involve negotiating flexible work arrangements or seeking support or resources to manage your workload.

Seek support: To manage your work-life balance, it's important to seek support from others. This might involve talking to a friend or family member, seeking support from a coach or mentor, or joining a support group.

Managing work-life balance requires a combination of boundary-setting, prioritization, delegation, self-care, communication, and support. By setting clear boundaries, prioritizing your commitments, delegating and outsourcing tasks, making time for self-care, communicating with your employer, and seeking support, you can improve your work-life balance and make time for the things that are most important to you.

Benefits of work-life balance

Improved productivity: Maintaining balance between work and personal life can help improve your productivity. When you have a healthy work-life balance, you are more likely to be focused and energized when you are working, and less likely to be burnt out or overwhelmed.

Reduced stress: Maintaining balance between work and personal life can help reduce stress and improve your overall well-being. When you have time for yourself and the things you enjoy outside of work, you can reduce the negative impact of stress on your health and well-being. The reduction in stress not only helps with your overall happiness levels but also helps with better productivity at work. Who knew?!

Better decision-making: Maintaining balance between work and personal life can also help improve your decision-making skills. When you are rested and not overwhelmed with work, you are more likely to be able to think clearly and make sound decisions.

Improved relationships: Maintaining balance between work and personal life can help improve your relationships with others. When you have time to spend with family and friends, you can strengthen your connections and improve your overall quality of life.

Increased happiness: Studies have shown that people who maintain balance between work and personal life tend to be happier and more satisfied with their lives overall. By prioritizing your well-being and the things you enjoy, you can increase your overall happiness and well-being.

Maintaining balance between work and personal life is important for your productivity, well-being, and overall quality of life. By making time for yourself and the things you enjoy, you can improve your productivity, reduce stress, make better decisions, improve your relationships, and increase your happiness.

Time management is the process of planning and organizing your time to make the most of your available time and increase your productivity. Effective time management involves setting clear goals, prioritizing tasks, minimizing distractions, and using scheduling and time blocking techniques.

There are many benefits of good time management, including increased productivity, reduced stress, improved decision-making, and improved relationships. To assess your current time management skills, it can be helpful to measure how you currently spend your time and identify common time wasters.

To improve your time management skills, you can set clear and specific goals, break down larger goals into smaller, more manageable tasks, and use techniques for prioritizing tasks. Scheduling and time blocking can be useful tools for managing your time and staying on track. It's important to balance structured and flexible time to allow for unexpected events and unexpected opportunities.

Procrastination is a common challenge when it comes to time management, and it can be overcome by setting clear goals, breaking tasks down into smaller steps, and using tools to block distractions. Managing distractions and interruptions is an important part of time management, and it can be achieved by setting boundaries, using tools to block distractions, creating a distraction-free environment, and avoiding multitasking.

Increasing efficiency and productivity involves identifying your goals, breaking tasks down into smaller steps, using scheduling and time blocking, minimizing distractions, and taking breaks and prioritizing self-care. Streamlining tasks and workflow involves identifying bottlenecks, automating repetitive tasks, simplifying processes, using templates and standardized documents, implementing a project management system, and seeking feedback.

Taking breaks and maintaining a healthy work-life balance are important for productivity, well-being, and overall quality of life. Strategies for managing work-life balance include setting clear boundaries, prioritizing commitments, delegating and outsourcing tasks, making time for self-care, communicating with your employer, and seeking support.

To conclude I would just like to say that I deeply understand how difficult and frustrating it is to not be able to accomplish the tasks you want to because of procrastination and just general poor time management. The goal of this book was not to convert you in to a productivity machine over night but to help you understand the core issues behind the problem and create actionable solutions that can have an immediate impact, however small that may be. If this book managed to help you become even a little bit better then I feel I have done my job successfully ☺